I0364454

This Book Belongs To:

Copyright © Teresa Rother
All rights reserved. No part of this publication may be reproduced, distributed, or transmitted in any form or by any means, including photocopy, recording, or other electronic or mechanical methods.

Dedication

This Prayer Journal is dedicated to all the people who want to write down aspects of their daily prayer life.

You are my inspiration for producing this book and I'm honored to be a part of your ongoing spiritual journey.

How to Use this Book

This Prayer Journal will help guide you through your faith walk and strengthen your journey with Christ.

Here are examples of information for you to fill in and write the details for your daily devotions.

Fill in the following information:

1. Date- record date
2. Today's Bible Verse- write down your daily scripture readings
3. Reflection- write down reflections for Bible verses, your spiritual relationship with God, and what's in your heart
4. I Am Thankful For- reflect and write down what you are grateful for
5. Dreams and Goals- journal what your hopes, goals, and dreams
6. Prayer Requests- write down any prayer requests
7. Prayers Answered- jot down all answered prayers and dreams that have been fulfilled

Date

Today's Bible Verse

Reflection

I Am Thankful For:

Dreams & Goals

Date

Today's Bible Verse

Reflection

I Am Thankful For:

Dreams & Goals

Prayer Requests

Prayers Answered

Date

Today's Bible Verse

Reflection

I Am Thankful For:

Dreams & Goals

Prayer Requests

Prayers Answered

Date

Today's Bible Verse

Reflection

I Am Thankful For:

Dreams & Goals

Date

Today's Bible Verse

Reflection

I Am Thankful For:

Dreams & Goals

Prayer Requests

Prayers Answered

Date

Today's Bible Verse

Reflection

I Am Thankful For:

Dreams & Goals

Prayer Requests

Prayers Answered

Date

Today's Bible Verse

Reflection

I Am Thankful For:

Dreams & Goals

Prayer Requests

Prayers Answered

Date

Today's Bible Verse

Reflection

I Am Thankful For:

Dreams & Goals

Date

Today's Bible Verse

Reflection

I Am Thankful For:

Dreams & Goals

Prayer Requests

Prayers Answered

Prayer Requests

Prayers Answered

Date

Today's Bible Verse

Reflection

I Am Thankful For:

Dreams & Goals

Date

Today's Bible Verse

Reflection

I Am Thankful For:

Dreams & Goals

Prayer Requests

Prayers Answered

Date

Today's Bible Verse

Reflection

I Am Thankful For:

Dreams & Goals

Prayer Requests

Prayers Answered

Date

Today's Bible Verse

Reflection

I Am Thankful For:

Dreams & Goals

Date

Today's Bible Verse

Reflection

I Am Thankful For:

Dreams & Goals

Date

Today's Bible Verse

Reflection

I Am Thankful For:

Dreams & Goals

Prayer Requests

Prayers Answered

Date

Today's Bible Verse

Reflection

I Am Thankful For:

Dreams & Goals

Prayer Requests

Prayers Answered

＝

Prayer Requests

Prayers Answered

Date

Today's Bible Verse

Reflection

I Am Thankful For:

Dreams & Goals

Date

Today's Bible Verse

Reflection

I Am Thankful For:

Dreams & Goals

Date

Today's Bible Verse

Reflection

I Am Thankful For:

Dreams & Goals

Date

Today's Bible Verse

Reflection

I Am Thankful For:

Dreams & Goals

Date

Today's Bible Verse

Reflection

I Am Thankful For:

Dreams
&
Goals

Prayer Requests

Prayers Answered

Date

Today's Bible Verse

Reflection

I Am Thankful For:

Dreams & Goals

Prayer Requests

Prayers Answered

Date

Today's Bible Verse

Reflection

I Am Thankful For:

Dreams & Goals

Date

Today's Bible Verse

Reflection

I Am Thankful For:

Dreams & Goals

Date

Today's Bible Verse

Reflection

I Am Thankful For:

Dreams & Goals

Prayer Requests

Prayers Answered

Prayer Requests

Prayers Answered

Date

Today's Bible Verse

Reflection

I Am Thankful For:

Dreams & Goals

Prayer Requests

Prayers Answered

Date

Today's Bible Verse

Reflection

I Am Thankful For:

Dreams & Goals

Prayer Requests

Prayers Answered

Date

Today's Bible Verse

Reflection

I Am Thankful For:

Dreams & Goals

Prayer Requests

Prayers Answered

Date

Today's Bible Verse

Reflection

I Am Thankful For:

Dreams & Goals

www.ingramcontent.com/pod-product-compliance
Lightning Source LLC
Chambersburg PA
CBHW052207090526
44583CB00017BA/2417